Leaves

by Grace Hansen

Abdo
PLANT ANATOMY
Kids

abdopublishing.com

Published by Abdo Kids, a division of ABDO, PO Box 398166, Minneapolis, Minnesota 55439.

Copyright © 2016 by Abdo Consulting Group, Inc. International copyrights reserved in all countries. No part of this book may be reproduced in any form without written permission from the publisher.

Printed in the United States of America, North Mankato, Minnesota.

102015

012016

THIS BOOK CONTAINS
RECYCLED MATERIALS

Photo Credits: iStock, Science Source, Shutterstock

Production Contributors: Teddy Borth, Jennie Forsberg, Grace Hansen

Design Contributors: Laura Mitchell, Dorothy Toth

Library of Congress Control Number: 2015942105

Cataloging-in-Publication Data

Hansen, Grace.

 Leaves / Grace Hansen.

  p. cm. -- (Plant anatomy)

ISBN 978-1-68080-137-8 (lib. bdg.)

Includes index.

1. Leaves--Juvenile literature.   I. Title.

575.5/7--dc23

                    2015942105

Table of Contents

Leaves

Leaves are parts of plants. They grow on the stems of flowers. They grow on trees. Leaves are on bushes and vines, too.

Nature's Chefs

Leaves are very important.

They make food for plants.

Leaves use the sun's light to make food. This is called **photosynthesis**.

Leaves are green.

This is because of

chlorophyll. It makes

photosynthesis possible.

Leaves also need **carbon dioxide** to make food. They get it from the air. They need water, too.

12

13

There are small openings on leaves. They are called stomata. Stomata let air and water in and out.

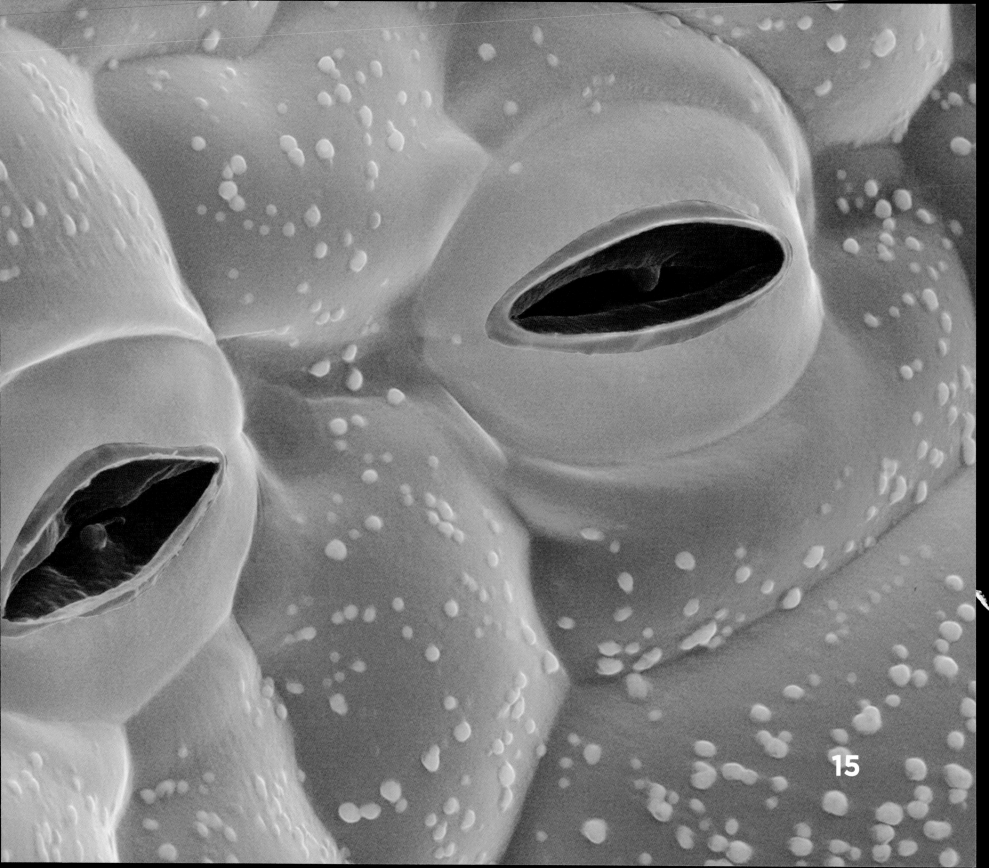

15

Letting water out is called transpiration. Summer can be hot. Wet leaves help plants stay cool.

Preparing for Winter

Letting water out in winter is not good. Trees and bushes shed their leaves. This helps store water so they can survive.

19

Evergreen trees do not shed their leaves. Pine trees have leaves called needles. Needles have wax on them. Wax helps the needles store water.

Leaf Anatomy

Blade

Vein

Midrib

Petriole

Glossary

carbon dioxide – a colorless gas that is absorbed from the air by plants in photosynthesis.

chlorophyll – the green matter of certain plants that absorbs light and is necessary for photosynthesis.

photosynthesis – the process that plants use to make food with air, water, and light.

Index

abdokids.com

Use this code to log on to abdokids.com and access crafts, games, videos, and more!

Abdo Kids Code:
PLK1378

DATE DUE

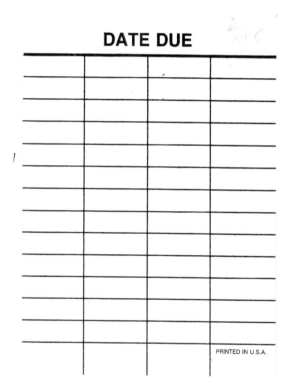

PRINTED IN U.S.A.